I AM HER TRIBE

I AM HER TRIBE

DANIELLE DOBY

Andrews McMeel
PUBLISHING®

for the seekers.
keep choosing in the name of your heart.

come as you are.
your breath can rest here.

this is a story of becoming.

the invitation

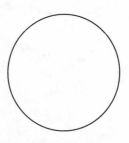

a hymnal to my younger self

one day you will awake with the craving for self-discovery.
when this knowing arrives,
and you feel the pull to go out into the world,
my hope for you is that your story begins
on the cool wood of your kitchen floor.

you
bare-skinned.
sitting down.
both eyes closed.
one hand on heart.
the other resting on your soft belly.

this.
this connection right here.
is the wisdom of the women before you.
and the tender infinite living within you.
and if there is ever a time you feel lost outside of yourself,
these guiding forces will always bring you back home.

my hope for you
is that you trust the teachings of what brings discomfort.
that when you feel as if you are at the cusp of breaking open,
out into the wild of the unknown,
you step forward with both feet planted
in your curiosity and wonder.

my hope for you
is that you greet your reflection with kind eyes.
that you never look to someone else for your belonging.
always moving from a space of worthiness,
longing for nothing of addition or subtraction.

my hope for you
is that you never stifle in your own power.
may you always carry the belief that your words matter.
unafraid to sing your truth at the tip-top of your lungs.

my hope for you
is that you honor each moment in its entirety.
that you choose your feeling over being numb + disconnected.
owning every curve of life's light and shadow sensations.
for you understand that in the present moment is where your
happiness is found.

this.
this is my hope for you.

some days there is a pull
for something more
a glimpse
of a distant vision
that is just fingertip
out of reach

it's as if my soul knows
i can no longer be held
by the earth i stand on

my feet
grown too large
my cheek
unable to feel
the warmth of the sun

i find myself moving
in daydreams

drifting between
here
and what could be

what is known
and what is becoming

though it offers movement
swaying in the center
does not bring
heart fulfillment

so i must go
i must move forward
i must open
these palms wide
to a life that has yet
to be awakened

leaves
energy
the shifting
between space + season
it's all movement
into what's new
and possible

do not fast forward
into something
you're not ready for

or allow yourself
to shrink back
into what's comfortable

growth lives in
the uneasiness
the in-between
the unfinished sentence

you are a
season of becoming

the clearing

if what you say
and what you do
aren't adding up
look for the fear
and look at it
closely

what is real here
in these words of yours?

what choice
can you make
to move into right now

so you can do something
you haven't done before?

feel something
you haven't felt before?

be something
you've never been before?

be here, now.

lately
i have found myself wanting to rush
my way to the ending of things

interactions
experiences
feelings
silence

right now
i am in the practice of not pushing so hard

rather
dropping back into my body

taking the extra moments
to really feel my feet
on the ground

and being with my breath
and what i find there
in its wholeness

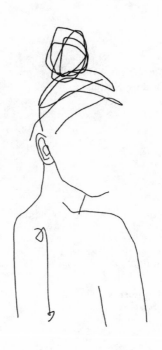

feelings

the ones that swallow
the ones that hollow
the ones that lift
cleanse
tighten
and expand

each one is sacred

each one

a messenger

honor the courage
it takes to travel this far

as they
are moving you
closer

to you

i am a runner.

i run from silence.
from difficult conversations.
from my truth.
even from love, unless i catch myself.

i choose to give + give
before receiving.

i will bury myself into the ground
with "i am fine"
until my body stops me.

it is a daily choice
in my practice
to choose to lean in closer,
instead of turning a cheek,
to what doesn't come easy for me.

this is why art,
my creative process,
is so important for me + my growth.

it asks of me to be willing.

am i willing to sit with
the hurt.
the healed.
the loud.
the quiet.
the yet to be spoken.
and let their stories rise up
out of me
for others to see.
and read.
and digest.
and form an experience of?

it is such a push + pull feeling
owning a heart
that wants to break open
and close off simultaneously.

the goosebumps.
the tingling.
the ache to run.
only confirm
what a holy act of courage it is
when we birth our art into the world.

when we risk comfort
we open up the doorway
to invite really good things
into our lives.

we begin by being willing.

the gateway

our practice of cultivating stillness
is just as important to our growth
as our momentum is

we say we want change
and so
we must take the time to stop
and ask the questions

what's working?
what's blocking?
where can i let go
and make room
for what's making its way to me?

it's never too late
to push pause
disrupt the plan
or choose an entirely new path

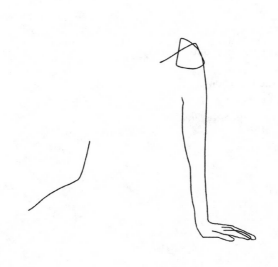

a certain freedom
is awakened
when we choose
to meet our fear
with compassion
and
worthiness

it took me a long time
to create an earth
that would hold me
for all that i am

a world
where i felt safe
to release the armor
of pretending
that was keeping
my truest light
from being seen
or touched

for every layer
i peeled back
was met with
fear + resistance

but as i continued
to turn inward
the stories
began to burn
and fall
from my body

it was there
underneath the confusion
i found
the beautiful mystery
of forgiveness + belonging

the beautiful thing
about being in the mess
is

it creates friction
it shakes comfort
it ignites movement

movement
if we let it
helps us sift through
what's real
what's of value
and
what deserves to stay

the water that opens you

what would it feel like to come undone?

to not fasten down
but let yourself flood?

to not close
but open yourself to
experience it all?

what would it feel like to come undone?

to move past your edge
instead of run?

to lose your fear
and meet the quiet depths within?

what would it feel like to come undone?

to release the weight
and find your freedom?

the cleansing has come
to bring you back home
to you.

you deserve
to live a life
with ease

as simple
light
and complicated
as that may
feel

what if it was meant
to be this fluid?

as the ocean says

the struggle
softens

the tearing
opens

remain present to it

it's all an invitation.

the aching

you are a match for your mountain.

the earth that holds you

i know some days the light
can seem too far out of reach
and there are some nights
when you can barely breathe
the flowers in your eyes
wilting one by one
then dropping to the floor

our healing isn't always
meant to be seen
sometimes it is
stepping foot into the forest
carving the sacred
out of our darkness

the aching
has her teachings
and when we get quiet enough
we hear its stories
the answers have always been
buried deep within
the shadows of our ground

come softly
sit quietly
and lean in closer

do not be scared
of the dark

of your dark

it is where your growth lives

in time
your eyes will bloom
again

give yourself
permission
to be where
you are

and
to still be loved
for it

for as long as i can remember
i have been at war with my own body.

i have starved it.
i have shamed it.
i have numbed it.
i have punished it.
i have abandoned it.
i have given away its power.

i am still learning.
daily.
how to return to myself.

every morning when i wake up
before i choose to go out + meet the world
i turn on music and move.

i move freely.
in an expansion.
not caring what it looks like.
and with only one intention.

to feel something.

to connect to the one thing
i have spent so long
trying to disconnect from.

it's only
and
ever
heart work.

weathered silk

it's 2 p.m. on a wednesday afternoon
the palo santo is burning
my shadow is dancing
as i make my way through
the house

this is an apology
to myself
for the shame i carried
because i never stopped loving you

our transformation is not always loud + arrow fast

sometimes it's years later
you're standing there
when your jaw softens
and you realize
you're no longer the same
as when you first walked in

where you were once closed
you have now let yourself slowly fold open

where you were once hardened
you have now become weathered silk + see-through

it is okay to be here
it is okay to not rush through and destroy your middle

the place where you reach for the future
just before you shed yourself of the past

each valley holds rich value
each in-between gifts you the resilience
to greet what's next

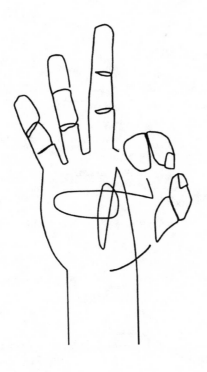

light alchemy

to be in the work of our shadow
is to be in the work of what's sacred.

honor this work.

the breaking
leads to opening

the opening
allows expansion

the expansion
creates more space

the space
invites growth in

the sound of sacred

have you ever reached your hands out into receiving
and heard the faint voice of your chest popping?

for me, it's the sound of sacred.

for me, it's the sound of expansion.
an opening being created.

it's like the morning sun
trying to dance its way through
the linen curtains — a light rising to be felt.

laughter at 3 a.m. on the kitchen floor.

a crimson pause
before the moon shows herself.

the nights spent awake crying
as you learn to sleep
in the middle of your bed again.

our work is to remember
that this
too
is sacred.

the extreme highs
and the low lows
are just as necessary for our growth
as food
water
shelter
and the entire horizon line.

each one creates movement.
a breaking.
a ground that invites more feeling to enter.

wherever you are.

in your high
or your low.

keep your hands
moving against the walls
to find the break.
the discomfort.
the aliveness
of it all.

goodness awaits you.

do not break
to break down.

break
to break open.

we cannot truly
grasp the depth
of our light

until
we are shown
our darkness

to clear the river

friction doesn't have to be
some dark + scary thing
we should avoid eye contact with

without it
there would be no change

friction is what pulls our greatness
out from under the sheets
it calls us from our
darkest corners of hiding
and invites us to grow
from our broken cracks + crevices

sometimes
this looks like letting go

and sometimes
even
letting in

friction breaks our hearts open
to a new capacity for receiving

it brings us down
to our knees of clarity
allowing us to gather
what is left in our hands
only opening our palms wide enough
to hold what's of value
and in alignment with
who we are now

and here
after we have cleared the river
we emerge into a being
that is softer
stronger
more loving
and grateful

it is our most
challenging seasons
that serve as
our greatest teachers

we must trust
that when people hurt us
we have served them
and their growth
somehow.

we are not in control
of what lessons
others are here
to learn.

their journey
wasn't ever ours to take.

it isn't ours
to carry the weight of.

i hate
that i cannot heal you.

all i can do
is love you.

letting that be enough
is a lesson
you knew i needed
to learn.

i hate
that i cannot thank you.

there is no grace here
yet
for you to know.

i know what it means
to feel things in oceans

i know what it means
to have a heart
that would drown itself
for others
before the need
to surface for air

when you feel things deeply
every fall
every cut
every word
consumes
and carves
a new world from within

every
i am sorry
please forgive me
it won't happen again
becomes full + round
with sunlight
and promise

my heart
travels between the freedom to go
and the urge to stay

he is a beautiful man i am in love with

he is a beautiful man i am afraid of

here i stand
arms cradling your red flags

and here you are
tight fist
and mouthful of broken promise

would i even know abuse
if it were called out by name?

when did i become a less i?

and when did our love
become a more mountain you?

to have your heart exist
inside someone else's chest
bruised
bloodied
and starved to the bone
how can one still know this as home?

i taste the alarms in the air between us
warning lights flashing within hands' reach
yet still
my jaw will not open
to claim their existence

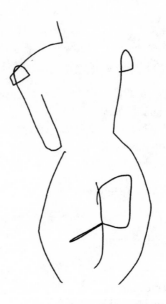

my thighs
have been forced open
to men of pain
men of shame

rage
pouring from their eyes

when night arrives
my chest warms
and i begin to burn

i reach for the glass
open my mouth
and try to drown
their memory
from the inside out

i am slowly learning
that flooding
the moons
brings no rest
to what they left behind

a virgo
no longer a virgin
you took that away
from me

you gifted me
the scarlet letter

a capital S shame
and buried it deep
within my garden

never to give rise
or bloom
to anything but vines

twisted
rooted
slowly cutting off
my air supply

when did no
mean yes
and yes
mean yes
with fear disguised
as shallow laughter

pushing your hands away

your body hovering
like a second skin
i couldn't cut off me

was it the short dress?
her playful gaze?
she must have asked for it
is the burden i wear
for others to excuse this

why are we so quick
to dismiss
the mouths of girls?

as if they are
too soft
too malleable
too fragile
too unknowing
of the world + how love works?

i am told he didn't mean it

will anyone believe me?

unspoken words
become the concrete in our throats

but even against the weight of cement
flowers will grow

you push aside a voice
for so long
that its whisper
becomes a muffle

a muffle
becomes a rumble
becomes a roar

one after another
a chorus of women
rising together

coming out of the shadows
to rewrite the untold stories of our daughters

lighting the path to a future
where no one has to say "me, too" again

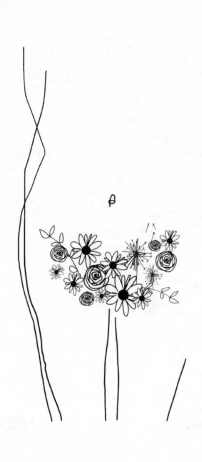

the heaviness
is here
to teach you
how to rise
again

the return

you were heavy.
and i needed you to be.

i needed you to weigh me down
into the ground so hard
that i was forced
to let go of some things.

expectations.
loss.
planned futures.
the pain that harbors
underneath my left shoulder blade
where i keep my heartbreak
alive + well with me.

transformation is a dark
muddy river
that isn't breezily navigated.

all we can do
is keep putting one foot
in front of the other
out into the unknown
and hope that we are grounded enough
to catch ourselves when we fall.

letting go
isn't something we can sail through
like clear waters.

it isn't something we can
shame into a small existence.

it isn't ignoring.
shoving aside.
or repeating the lyrics
"it doesn't matter, i am just fine."

i quit telling myself that story.
so i went out and wrote a new one.

instead
i choose the story of being.

to be with myself.
my alone.
my pain.
my experience.
not numb.
not hide.
not run.
because
oh
sometimes do i want to run.

i choose to be.

and it's when i honor this pain.
when i give it the room to breathe
and simply be
that's the moment i invite
love to be
too.

undressed

it's
when i slowed down
in a space of reflection
i realized that
i couldn't save myself
by focusing on
trying to save others

my work
my healing
was only + ever
going to begin
with myself

people tend to not move
out of their pain
because at least they know
what they are getting

our attachment to pain
is fascinating to me

what i have found
through my own process
is that my pain
was
and still is
the biggest catalyst
for change in my life

if i were to deny myself
of its momentum
out of fear
of what moving through it
might bring

i would only be settling
for what's known
and comfortable

i would only be settling
for a life
that is less
than i am capable of creating

do not skip
the
struggle.

come as you are

the light in me
cannot always see + honor the light in you.

and it's because of this.
the love of the process.
the love of this journey.
i keep showing up to practice.

for me,
it's all yoga.

finding steady breath in the unknown.
the rhythmic flow when words fall off my tongue
and down onto paper.
granting myself permission to say no — without apology.
grounding my feet into the space that was created
after he left me.

all is not right.

nor wrong.

it just is.

lessons worth learning
and relearning —

none of this was meant to be done all alone.
there is nothing courageous about covering up
your pain so no one sees it.
there is nothing glorified about having it all together.
you do not need to justify choosing your health
over someone's happiness or approval.
and life can be wonderful.
perfect.
even when
and especially when
it's hard.

craft magic
out of your tragedies
and use the strength
of your story
to bring you closer to love

not further away from it

the dark
has weathered me
to a place of tenderness

and heart space

and then i surrendered.
to the soft.
and the sweet.
and the sorrow.

not shying away.
allowing each inhale + exhale to source a new life
in my cells from their exchange.

let this teach you.

within each release, lives an offering.
what we let go of, creates room for beginnings.
the morning light,
as white as the sheets that surround me,
now begins to lift the hole in my chest
where our love used to be.

let this teach you.

you cannot force a heart to dance with forgiveness.
only softness serves as the bridge to the divine.

your winter may last
for days.
months.
lifetimes.
but do not mistake this as a dead bloom.
forever closed off to others.

for this season isn't for rising, just yet.
this season is for letting the light
pour itself
into our emptied hands.

let this teach you.

the nectar

for you

some nights when i cannot sleep
i find myself dreaming of what you will be like

your dark hair
coffee stained t-shirt
and laugh lines from a life lived full + well

i turn to you
your hands resting at the tip of my hips
you pull me in. closer.
gentle. like water.
we do not have to mold
or fold
or move our bodies
into places they do not want to belong
i hold my breath
for just a few moments longer
so this feeling will land

i believe you can manifest others into your existence

i believe that the valley of our chest
serves as a soft landing for our blessings

i believe that past heartbreak moves us closer
to meeting this love — a love that awakens us

i believe there are other open oceans that are ready + willing
we just need to keep the dream alive to them

as i drift back to sleep
i place my hand upon my heart — the space where all resides

dear universe
dear all that is holy + divine
please keep him safe
and remind him that he is loved
as he makes his way here to me

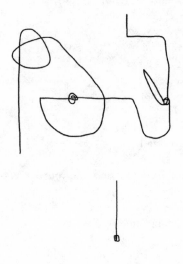

fall hard
and often.

there is beauty
in the heart's gravity.

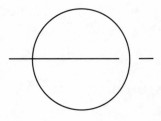

soft magic

i can fall in love within moments of meeting someone.

when the truest self is revealed
the line blurs between seconds and lifetimes.
our stories tethered.
alive in the marrow.
it's as if i have known you all along — because i have.

love mirrors.
and it moves.
it's circular.
uniting you at your edges.

my ability to love deep
and freely
is something i will not ever
try to shame or dishonor.

i would rather be open to a love
that is short-lived and consuming.

one that breathes me wide awake.

not a shackled life
constrained by my very own resistance.

afraid to feel anything
other than shallow waters.

i would rather risk
by wading my way out to it.

stepping into
an unknown depth.

i will not let
my grip on safety
carve its quiet desert
from within.

to feel something

i am the reason you have eighteen different smiles
one for when he walks into the room

i am every penny you have ever wished on
the silence that stands between you and a sunset
the tingle you feel when your hand fits perfectly
in the cusp of another's

i am laughter at 4 a.m. on the kitchen floor
the reason you choose sunflowers over tulips
the rhythm of rain that plays the soundtrack
to your perfect sunday morning

i am the tears that stain your satin pillow
the fire in your belly when you speak your truth
the deep exhale when you hear the words "hey, me too"

i am the only thing that breaks
just to get bigger

i am your heart

and i am here to make you feel something

the why of the way

your true north
is also the direction of love

watch where your heart
gravitates to

i want to be consumed by love

the kind of consumption like that of sunlight
its warmth honors my wild
and fuels my freedom
holding me for all that i am
for it knows that even
the darkest parts of me
hold a shine to them
that won't ever fade away

i am done hiding from you
i am finished playing musical chairs
with reasons not to try again

i crave to go higher
come take me higher
push me to expand beyond myself
out into what's possible
so that i can feel something
i haven't felt before

let me write my story
through the very tips of my toes
that i travel on
giving me room to breathe
and create
yet to always find
my way back home
in the nook of your left shoulder

mornings with tangled limbs
linen sheets
and the smell of the sky falling
outside our open windows
3 a.m. conversations
about your deepest fears
and mid-sentence stops
to dance barefoot in the kitchen
just because

come honor me
in my wholeness
both the tall parts
and the messy parts

invite me to rise into
the parts of me
that still need growing

i want to do the work with you
i want to co-create with you

together
taking each other
to a bigger version of ourselves
that we cannot reach
all on our own

before you
i have crashed
and i have burned

but this burn taught me
that love
real love
awakens when we choose
to meet ourselves

this burn taught me
that i will find you
and i will love you

because i did the work
to find + love me, too

our story has a pulse

to be in his presence is
a poem
a sermon
a full body prayer

i choose
full on
full grasp
full moon

love
in its fullest circle

i do not know
how to love
in moderation

my heart breathes
a gentle intensity

for eyes that bloom

do not come to me
with a love
that is tongue-tied
of desert thirst
only half-exposed

my hands
can only grasp
what is
full breath
strong pulse
and intoxicating

anything less
will not bring
my heart
to its knees

open heart.
with backbone.

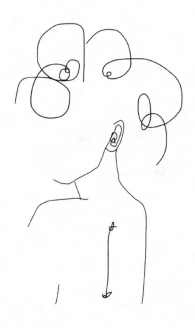

half-heartedness
isn't an ingredient for my existence.

i crave a life of magic.

stop.
stand here.
and breathe in
all that makes you grateful for this life.

a good laugh.
a good cry.
when both are fused together
at the same time.

soul connections.
choosing someone with your whole heart.
the ease exhaled after the release.

tuck these close
into the corners of your pockets.

the deep crevices of your spine.

so you may always
stand tall in the belief
that no matter what you are given
magic is always present within you
in what's here
and what's right now.

you are worth finding
worth knowing
worth loving

you and all your one million layers

each day
i am learning
to keep leaning
into the broken crack
of my chest

because it's here
in this space of expanding
i will keep making room
for the adventure
that will be you
one day

let your heart break daily

in conversations
over song lyrics
during the pause right before the sun rises
while you're sipping coffee
and looking into the eyes
of someone you love

for it's when we break a little
we come alive

it's in this space of feeling
we expand

and it's here
in our vulnerability and openness
we step into our greatest selves

quit hiding your magic.
the world is ready
for you.

the rise

the fire that awakens you

i am drawn to the light in others
it is how i know i am not alone

to be a seeker of the light
is to be connected to the very truth itself —

    the way out of the darkness
    is when we can look across the table
    and find our face in another's

when we let our stories exist
we invite others to see themselves more clearly
in a space where
pain
struggle
stunning resilience
and belonging
are not unique to just one person

they live in each of us
proving we are not on our own

i heal
and you heal
and when we heal
the world heals with us

an open heart is the key
that unlocks hope's reach

the sun is here
within you
now open your eyes

you just need to be willing

to fail
to feel
to heal
to forgive
to forgive
to forgive
to forgive
and to love

again

we learn

compassion
through hardship

gratitude
through absence

wisdom
through our experiences

we become teachers
by first
being a student

trust that every no
every rejection
is all a part of the invitation

it is a redirection to
a higher purpose

it is the universe guiding us
into the bigger story
our past has prepared us for

when you make things
break things
mend things
love + leave things
it keeps you moving forward
down your own meandering path

and as the scenery shifts
so will you

then one day
without heart's notice
you will find you have arrived

i promise you
your greatest growth
cannot be found in your knowing

your revolution
is waiting for you
in the pieces you have yet
to make known + discover

within each moment
lives the fresh opportunity
to breathe new life
into who you want to be

two feet in

this year
i choose to burn my good candles
on a tuesday at noon
just because
i choose to use the expensive lotion
the one i keep tucked safe up on the counter
not ration any of my most cherished belongings
because i am worth investing in — right now

this year
i choose to wear that thing
you know
the one i told myself i would slip on
when i looked a certain way?
i choose to love my body
this vessel i have been given
and her seasons as they shift

this year
i give myself permission to change
and keep changing
for i understand
there is an underlying truth when it comes
to becoming — it doesn't have to mirror anyone else

this year
i choose to let go
really let go
of the heavy
of the half-hearted
no more forcing connection
where it no longer lives
i choose to nourish
what's willing to grow

this year
i choose to be grateful
for the teachings of my yesterday
i honor my wholeness
when i honor my whole story — even the shaky parts

this year
i choose to step forward

clear eyes
heart open
two feet grounded

palms wide
to the all-is-possible
unknown
and new

the distance of possibility

your freedom lives
in your ability to understand
that nothing is certain
yet
in the uncertainty
you hold the power
to create anything

give your desires a voice

instead of thinking
     what could go wrong
     what you could lose
     or how it might feel

declare what it is you want to happen

a power lives in our ability
to say what we want

and to believe we are worthy of it

there is no magic
to be found
in using only a fraction
of your heart space

mirror work

how you choose to show up
magnetizes what shows up for you

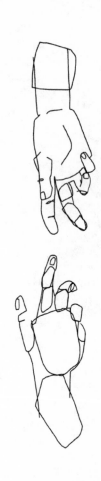

the air that moves you

we are always in transition

stretching
reaching
growing at our edges

one day we will wake up
and reveal the truth

that none of this is permanent
all is temporary
and the time for forgiveness
has always been now

so move through your blocking

release
what keeps you tethered
to the ground

step out of comparison
and open your palms
to your own unique
brilliant experience

the one that is unfolding
just for you — because it is

for it's in the unknown
we find a deeper understanding

we come alive
in the mystery of it all

move your feet
move your mind
move your mountains
to show others
they can climb

move forward
move freely
move
me

find what ignites worlds within you

let your work
everything you create
be a direct extension of
your heart space

now
more than ever
the world needs more of our light

go find what sparks it
and people who wholeheartedly
believe in it

and use it to go out + change something

ripples

when you create a difference
in someone's life
you not only impact their life
you impact everyone influenced by them
throughout their entire lifetime

no act is ever too small

one by one
this is how to make an ocean rise

heart work

your purpose
your art
will land in the hearts
it's meant to

you won't be for everyone

but you are for someone

and to that someone
what you have to give matters

and that's the beginning
of everything

nourishment

be selective
in what words
you choose to ingest

both
from yourself
and others

shifting tides

a fine line exists
between adaptability
and sacrificing self

know when
you go with the flow
and when
you give your flow away

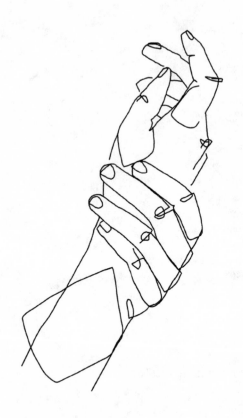

stop and inhale

it is unsustainable
to give
and give
and give
until you have nothing left

before you hit empty
you will be offering something
that isn't even real

the practice | *freedom*

i am not in control of what lessons
others are here to learn

i am not in control of what lessons
others are here to teach me

when i try to control
when i try to tight grasp
when i try to bend + force
and push others somewhere
they are not ready for

or maybe, do not even belong

i separate myself from trusting in the nature of all

that all is given
to bring us closer to love
all is given
to call us back home

the practice | *letting go*

my strength is not determined
by the heaviness i choose to carry

when i loosen my grip on what once was
i allow myself to experience the fullness of what is now

when i release what no longer serves me
i return to the natural rhythm of my highest Self

to be connected to Self
is to be connected to the very ground
i stand on — the foundation where all rises from

my past does not define all that i am
it waters my roots + prepares me for where i am going

the practice | *wonder*

i am still learning

when i am able to move from a space of inquiry
within the world around me
instead from a place of all-knowing
i open up the possibility to invite growth in

i do not allow my anxiety to consume me
for not having all of the answers

i know that fear craves certainty and safety
and something concrete

i trust the freedom living in the unknown

it's there
in this wide open space
i hold the power to create something
that has yet to exist

the practice | *sacred spaces*

i am a safe landing for others

i embody

presence
clear of judgment

connection
over competition

support
without expectation

when i hold this space for someone
i send them the message that they matter
just as they are

my heart serves as an invitation
for others to show up + share
their brightest, most authentic light

what a gift i give to this world
when i choose to remain open

the practice | *fluidity*

i am sensual. tender. and round with aliveness.

i feel
i yearn
i learn

i heal

my ability to feel is what makes me beautiful

every feeling that visits me holds a story worth listening to
every feeling is an opening that helps me connect
to the deepest, truest parts of myself

i honor the rise + fall of my feelings
without numbing or resisting their teachings

i am a clear channel
tending to the fluid movement
of my own river of emotional expression

when i block myself from feeling
i deny myself the experience of what it means to be human

the practice | *self loving*

i am in love with the sound of my solitude
my alone is the greatest gift i can offer myself

the relationship i have with Self is a sacred one
for it is the soil all connection will bloom from

being in the work of belonging
teaches me that i cannot use other people
as a means of escape from my pain or my past

the work teaches me
that the key to infinite love
is when i crack my chest open wide enough
to invite myself to come back in

i do not wait on others to choose me
i take control of what it means to belong
when i choose myself, first

the practice | *body talk*

i will not mold + fold myself
in the name of beauty

every curve?
i call out sacred

every blemish?
i see a story

there is nothing small or delicate
about a woman's voice asking for forgiveness from her body

the undoing is a process
and freedom awaits me on the other side

i am real like the crease of my lips

i am real like the curves that i sway from

i am real like the stars that sing to you each night
only i am more beautiful

the sacred

the unlearning

this morning
i stepped out of the shower
and caught my reflection singing back at me

two eyes of evergreen
bare shoulders
and dark hair
carving its rivers down my naked limbs

they say healing begins
the moment a woman
can look into a mirror
and not clench her teeth down

do you want to know what beauty is?
come
and hold the curves of your body

do you want to know what wisdom is?
come
and journey the lines of your face

do you want to know what freedom is?
come
and let go of the stories they told you

to heal a war
is to look deeply into the eyes of another
and not turn away from what is found there

when you want to run
stay with the girl in the mirror
a few moments longer

a new world can awaken
within one shared breath

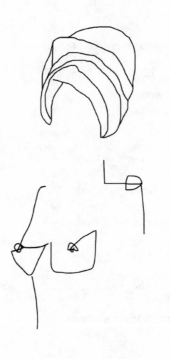

just as the moon
i am still learning
to stand fully
in my whole power

softness
with strength

sexual
still spiritual

independent
yet connected

deeply rooted
but free

flawed
and sacred

i am a woman of many shades
who i am is for me to define

i carry layers of imperfection

that
when woven together
create the hue
of my wholeness

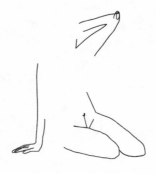

wild woman

the time has come for you to step forward, wild woman.
it is time for you to climb + claw your way out from your deepest
shadows of hiding.

can't you hear their call?

you have been deliberately forged from the dreams of your
ancestors, wild woman. their legacy has watered the earth you
will continue to rise from.

awaken to your voice.
your truth.
your belonging.
let your song make its way to the surface to breathe — for this is
an offering that only you can bring forth to the world.

can you meet your courage at its edge?

when all seems lost and suffocating,
do not abandon yourself, wild woman.
do not abandon your shake or your rumble.
your thirst or your hunger.
they exist to show you you've tried something.
loved something.
braved something.
longed for something worth fighting for.

bring with you your hurt, your sorrow, your burn that you carry.
unleash its scorch without fear of what comfort it may challenge.
just as you, it does not need permission to exist here.

the time has come for you to work through your aching, wild
woman. once you can do this, you can sit with the pains of
another — and not become them.

your strength is not defined by the heaviness you rest upon your
shoulders, wild woman. surrender it outside of yourself, for when
the heart is broken open the sweetness makes its way in.

you are anchored to the moon herself. you bring the unveiling
with you into the darkness. when the mask falls, and the forcing
fades, the light pours in and begins to show us the way.

the time has come for you to join hands with your sisters, wild
woman. the women of your yesterday, today and tomorrow.

honoring this union, this stretch of wisdom and story that flows
throughout time, gives us clues to where we are going. it shows
us that when we stand up together, when we step forward out
of the shadows, together, our voices become the bridge to a new
day's horizon.

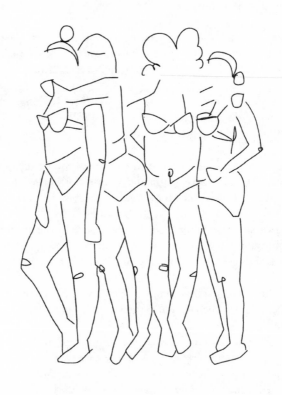

what is the quickest way for me to disconnect from my source?
comparison.

for a large part of my life i didn't have the healthiest relationship
when it came to women.

i viewed every experience through the lens of competition, and
would push aside my power the second i didn't feel worthy of my
surroundings.

i built a high fence around my heart to keep others out, yet lived
in the irony of desperately wanting to belong.

today,
i am still learning what it means to belong.
to myself.
and here.
with you.
in this very moment.

when i get scared,
when i feel as though i am sharing too much,
i remind myself to stay open.
to keep choosing this work.
for it's through this space that my vulnerability has created;
i have called in some of my most cherished female connections.

the best piece of relationship advice i have ever received?
find someone you want to do the work with.

our world expands when women show up to be in the work,
together. women who unapologetically own their independence,
yet still believe that the collective's success is just as important
and beautiful as their very own.

be grateful for your mirrors
your teachers
the technicolored souls in your life
that pull you out from your nest of hiding
because they believe in
the wild possibility
that is you in this world

these people will
push you
break you
mend you
love you
save you
and inspire you to keep reaching for more

standing on the shoulders of giants

to the women before me
thank you for leading the way

thank you for using your voice
to carve out room for mine to exist

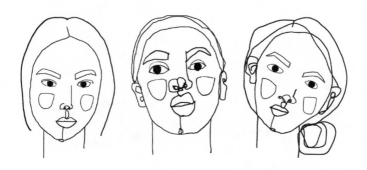

today and every day
i march for you

i march for you
because you are her
i am her
and she is her, too

i will not apologize
for my heart
my fire
divine power
or tender softness

these forces
catapult the universe
into a forward motion

both soft + fierce
can coexist
and still be powerful

my curves
are not an invitation
for you

my body is sacred
a temple to be worshipped

i am a woman
the force of life

i am worthy
of my deepest desires

do not ever
plant the core
of you
in another

you
are your sun

your
own center of gravity

you
rise
and fall
for you

the alchemy

the universe within

you are the
breath
river
ember
and root

let me remind you
dear one
of your elemental power

you are connected
to the very source
of all that surrounds you

aries

mar 21 — apr 19

i am her.

ruled by the planet of passion, her story is one of action,
direction + movement

she does not wait on the voice of permission to be smart,
strong or beautiful. she knows that only she gets to write the rules
on what it means to be a force in this world.

a flash of light. a one-way street. bow + arrow.
she is the stereo turned up. a new mountain to climb.
pushing herself and others outside of comfort zones.

with bravery coursing through her veins,
power pulsing at the curve of her hips,
she takes bold leaps + believes she will succeed in them.

head. and heart. she is a wildfire. a train at full speed.
she is not scared to work for her growth,
so she welcomes the unknown.
knowing it's here, where anything is possible,
she crafts her best life — the one of her dreams.

taurus

apr 20 — may 20

i am her.

she is ruled by the earth element and her practical nature.
a duality of both solid ground + tenderness.
an open heart with strong boundaries.

a devoted friend. a trust fall. your voice of reason.
she is a work of art. a garden growing. a deep exhale.

she will carry your love with an open palm.
unconditional is how you call her name.
only searching for what's real, full breath + consuming.
she knows there is no brilliance to be found in the half-hearted.

tangled in satin sheets. the taste of honey.
a familiar touch of an old book running along her fingertips.
a life adorned, these are the building blocks to her universe.

she notices the simple things,
revealing the beauty in what surrounds her.
she nourishes her dreams by honoring each moment
and the soft magic they inspire.

gemini

may 21 — jun 20

i am her.

governed by expression + her unbridled curiosity,
she greets each day with anticipation, eager to take on new roads
with her childlike wonder.

your first kiss. the scent of lavender.
she is twirling under the mother moon in crimson heels.
a forget-me-not. an open palm reaching.
she tucks away these treasured moments
in her back pocket for safekeeping.

she teaches us that when we do not explore different views,
we deny ourselves the richness of growth + experience.

so she chooses to answer the call for adventure
and wander off into the open wilderness.
the rebellion just outside the lines of what everyone else is doing.

the unknown is where she comes alive.
her courage illuminates her own trails.

cancer

jun 21 — jul 22

i am her.

she is a daughter of the moon.

*the way she moves, breathes + creates is all a direct
extension of her heart space. she feels things, deeply.
connected on a cellular level, a higher way of being.*

*as the moon turns, so does she. with each phase of its lunar cycle
revealing the shifting hues of her awakening.*

*a hand to hold. her grandmother's necklace. your morning coffee.
she is a fresh bloom. white linen sheets. a vivid daydream.*

*her love is both a solid ground and soft landing.
the meeting place of one's true vulnerability + innermost magic.*

*honoring both the light + the shadow,
she births a life that demands to be felt.
her beauty lives in her ability to heal others by healing herself.*

*a gentle intensity, governed by empathy,
her tenderness is what propels us forward.*

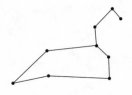

leo

jul 23 — aug 22

i am her.

daughter of the sun,
her story is one of passion, momentum + courage.
born from the fire with a purpose, on purpose,
she is a natural leader.

she reminds women of their lioness within,
digging her fingernails deep down into her truth + breathing
an arresting honesty into all she creates.

she is fierce. bold. and resilient.
she knows worthiness isn't something you go search for,
it is something you recognize you already are.

dark chocolate. warm embers. and backbone.
she is a big leap. a dream rising. a shade of something beautiful.

she opens her palms far and wide,
unafraid to take up space in this world.
she pushes the limits in the name of heart,
in the name of truth + what's possible.

virgo

aug 23 — sept 22

i am her.

ruled by the element earth and her structured creative messiness,
her story is one of detail, and bewilderment.
always observing, absorbing, greeting each feeling as though
she were meeting it for the very first time.

she is a seeker of goodness. in both herself and the world around her.
always inviting others to rise into the gifts they have to offer.

bare feet. palo santo. weathered books. the smell of cedar.
she is tender heart. written words. and dirty paintbrush water.

as she gets older, the stronger the call echoes for her to be outdoors.
to have the sun kiss her face. her naked limbs, skin on soil.
to remind her of the powerful connection she shares
with the earth she stands on.
her heart craves stillness, and grounding. so she offers her dreams
to be held amongst the trees, inhaling the sky's possibility + wonder.

it's here. in this space. she can breathe. deeply breathe.
and give her creativity the safe space to grow alongside her.

libra

sept 23 — oct 22

i am her.

guided by the element air, she is both the push + the pull,
a fluid dance between dark and light, her effort and ease.

soft, but not delicate. she is a peace keeper,
though unafraid to declare her truth for what she believes in.

a polished vase. vintage wine. the pages of her favorite book.
she is a loving gaze, the pause between dusk and day.
where the past lets go + steps into tomorrow.

her power lives in her ability to love and be loved in return.
her heart is ready. and willing. able to give freely.
and open to receiving.

she dreams of a love that will meet her halfway on the bridge.
a union that is honest, and equal. expansive, still grounded.
passionate, but gentle.

she views life through the lens of harmony + balance.
her spirit is something we all carry inside of ourselves.
the desire to let our hearts fall, yet still fly.

scorpio

oct 23 — nov 21

i am her.

*she will call you out of your darkest corners of hiding and invite
you to your edge — because she has seen what you are to become.*

*bone deep and exposed. her passion is contagious.
she is on a frequency all her own.*

*governed by water, she understands that all holds
great depth + value. all has a story worth listening to.*

*exotic. sensual. your darkest secret.
she is full grasp. a force of nature.
standing in her truth with both eyes open.*

*she is her own greatest dare.
following her courage over what's known + certain.
only watering beliefs that fuel her purpose.*

*even though her heart has been broken before,
she still sends it back out to brave love again.
she knows that in the risk, lives her untamed freedom.*

sagittarius

nov 22 — dec 21

i am her.

*ruled by the element fire and her constant craving for exploration
and open spaces, she is on a quest. a journey. writing her story
through the very tips of her toes she travels on.*

*as the scenery shifts, so does she.
as the miles roll on, so does her truth.
sometimes in silence. sometimes in laughter.
and sometimes on tear-stained paper.*

*she doesn't need a map to tell her where she is going,
for she knows when she follows her north,
it will always lead her back home.*

*passport stamps. seasons changing. a different view.
she is an open field. a curious mind. a seeker of her heart's truth.*

*adventure is her lover. experience, her teacher.
a wanderer of the world, finding healing in feeling.
she is expansion. untamed. and free.
born with a heart too big for only one city.*

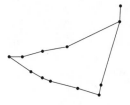

capricorn

dec 22 — jan 19

i am her.

*governed by earth, her deep rooting can weather life
and its stormy seasons, for she knows that with each setback,
there always comes a rising.*

*ruled by saturn, the planet of discipline, her story is one of structure,
stamina + dedication. where others may wither, she persists.
showing us that if we want to move forward,
we must first sit with the teachings of discomfort.*

*a lighthouse. winter flowers. her two feet in.
she is sturdy ground. eye contact. a ten-year vision.*

*she is a dichotomy, coming more alive as she ages.
with each mountain, she gains wisdom
through the valley of her experiences.*

*her commitment to the moment reveals an underlying truth,
that in order for us to access joy — one must be here,
right here + now.*

aquarius

jan 20 — feb 18

i am her.

she doesn't go with the flow. she is the flow.
her story is one of intellect and curiosity.
guided by feeling, she moves from a place of expansion.
always seeking honest spaces where her lungs can breathe
and she can share her truest self with those around her.

she's different. rare, even.
a cosmic rebellion interlaced with only good intentions.
she believes in the impact of her own momentum
and what her gifts can offer the world.

she will ask you what your heart longs for,
then help you find the courage within to go out + choose it.

the four winds. a cloud untamed. and self-expression.
she is a truth teller. a primal howl. an echo in the dark forest.

breaking away from the mundane,
you won't ever find her in stagnant water.
she is one for the changing tides, shifting patterns,
and shedding energy that is no longer aligned with her essence.

pisces

feb 19 — mar 20

i am her.

anchored by the stars in the open sky,
her hips sway to the beat of their own tempo.
her true nature is one of fluidity, emotional expression.

moved by neptune, the planet of dreams.
she is limitless, a giving heart, with no expectation of receiving.

in love with her own solitude, the universe within, she reminds us
that the bravest step one can take is by way of going inward.

walls down. a soft touch. the hum of her favorite song.
kind eyes. belly laughter. coffee conversations at the morning table.

her heart colors outside of its own lines,
letting its ink spill onto others' pages.
for she would rather feel this life than be disconnected from it.

knowing that no hands will ever be deep enough to hold her softness,
she continues to crack her chest open, leaving behind pieces
of it in everything she touches.

there is no greater love story
than you
in all that you are.

i hope you walk away
tall in the truth
that you are not alone.

You matter.
Your story matters.
Your feelings, ther matter.

hold that close. x

gratitude

to my parents, my reason. your love and sacrifice has watered the ground i will continue to rise from. i am, because you are.

to my nana, my muse. i am your revolution. your fire lives on in the sway of my hips and the ink from my fingertips.

to my sister, my teacher. you are honey. sunshine. and promise. thank you for showing me that in all lives a story, and value.

to lyndsey, shannon + jax, my coven. your love is a deep exhale. thank you for seeing me, and loving me, in all that i am.

to nova, my heart center. you are joy, in every shade of the word. how lucky we are that you chose us for this lifetime.

to chelsea, my creative force. you have brought these words to life with your hands. i am honored to share these pages with you.

to patty, tyler + Andrews McMeel Publishing, my answered prayer. thank you for believing in my voice and what this book has to offer the world.

to the readers, my mirrors. you have shown me the power in storytelling. thank you for holding the space for me to keep reaching, keep learning, keep sharing my journey.

Andrews McMeel Publishing
a division of Andrews McMeel Universal
1130 Walnut Street, Kansas City, Missouri 64106

www.andrewsmcmeel.com

18 19 20 21 22 BVG 10 9 8 7 6 5 4 3 2

ISBN: 978-1-4494-9555-8

Library of Congress Control Number: 2018950899

Editor: Patty Rice
Designer/Art Director: Julie Barnes
Production Editor: Dave Shaw
Production Manager: Cliff Koehler
Illustrations and Cover Design: Chelsea Leifken